CLASS 4

Ginger

Fit for five

Erarbeitet von
Wolfgang Gehring

Cornelsen

Contents

Me and my friends

1 Find 5 words and circle them. Look → and look ↓.

2 Write the words.

T	P	G	R	E	E	N	L
E	F	R	U	L	K	I	T
N	O	M	L	I	L	Y	K
N	N	K	O	N	R	I	S
I	T	K	L	D	O	G	K
S	E	N	P	L	I	N	R
E	N	G	L	A	N	D	T

Lily

 ____________

 ____________

 ____________

10 ____________

 ____________

3 Look at the crossword and complete the sentences.

4 Draw your friend.

Note:
she's = she is

Her name is Lily.

She's from ____________

She's ______ years old.

Her favourite sport is ____________

Her favourite colour is ____________

Her favourite pet is the ____________

Me and my friends

1 Complete the speech bubbles.

2 Glue on or draw the pictures.

3 Write the names.

Note:
I'm = I am

That's me.

My favourite colour is ____________

I'm from ____________

I'm ____ years old.

My favourite sport is ____________

name: ____________

That's my friend.

Her favourite colour is ____________

She's from ____________

She's ____ years old.

Her favourite sport is ____________

name: ____________

Me and my friends

1 Write the sentences.

2 Complete the speech bubbles. Look on page 3.

Note:
what's = what is

your / What's / name?

What's your name?

My name is Lily.

from / are / Where / you?

____

I'm from ______

old / How / you / are?

____

I'm _____ years old.

your / favourite / What's / sport?

____

____

favourite / What's / pet / your?

____

____

colour / What's / favourite / your?

____

____

3 Write one sentence about yourself.

____

____

My family

1 Find 5 words and circle them. Look → and look ↓.

2 Write the words.

U	I	D	O	P	G	X	H	I	M	P
S	W	J	S	B	R	O	T	H	E	R
I	P	A	X	F	A	T	H	E	R	H
S	B	T	N	M	N	E	R	Z	L	Z
T	G	R	A	N	D	P	A	H	P	B
E	U	A	K	O	M	O	T	H	E	R
R	U	M	A	K	A	J	O	D	E	X

father • mother • ~~grandpa~~
grandma • brother • sister

grandpa

____

____

____

____

____

Note:
grandpa = grandfather
grandma = grandmother

3 Look at Karen's family. Complete the sentences.

This is John, my grandpa.

This is Linda, my ______________

__________ Lucy, my ______________

__________ Bill, ______________

__________ Jenny, ______________

__________ Tom, ______________

__________ Emma, ______________

Hi, I'm Karen. ______________ family.

__________ Ben, ______________

My family

1 Tick the right answers.

	Yes	No
Bill is Karen's grandpa.	✓	
John is Karen's father.		
Emma is Karen's sister.		
Jenny is Karen's mother.		
Lucy is Karen's sister.		
Ben is Karen's brother.		

2 Make sentences about Karen's family. Draw lines.

Jenny
Bill
Lucy
Emma
Ben
Tom
Linda
John
Charlie

is Karen's

father
mother
sister
brother
grandpa
grandma
dog

3 He or she? Write the family words.

Note:
my dog Charlie = he
a dog = it

grandpa

___________________ ___________________

___________________ ___________________

___________________ ___________________

My family

1 Who is who in Karen's family? Look on page 6. Number the pictures.

2 Write the sentences.

1. This is my grandpa Bill. He's 65.
2. This is my ________ Emma. She's ________
3. ____________ father Tom. ____________________
4. ____________ grandma ____________________ 63.
5. ____ 32.
6. ______________________ Ben. ______________
7. ______________________ Linda. ____________
8. ____ 67.

3 Who is missing? Write the sentence and number the picture.

9. ______________________________

____

4 Complete the drawing.

My family

1 Find 5 words and colour them.

2 Write the words.

3 Do you know one more? Colour and write.

________ ________ ________ ________ ________ ________

4 Tick the right answers.

	bananas are yellow	shamrocks are green	cola is brown	the sun is blue	crocodiles are red
Yes	✓				
No					

5 Colour the pictures.

6 Write the sentences.

Note:
they are – they aren't
it is – it isn't

Yes, bananas are yellow.

No, ________ isn't blue. It is ________________

No, ____________ aren't red. ________________

Yes, ________________________

____

My family

1 Complete the sentences.

2 Write the numbers in the boxes.

under • on • behind • in
yellow • brown • pink • ~~black~~

(1) The black cat is ___________ the chair.

(2) The _________ cheese ____________ sandwich.

(3) ______________ dog ___________ ______ table.

(4) ____________ flower ____________ glass.

3 Match the sentences. Draw lines.

Sage, dass deine Mutter 32 Jahre alt ist.

Sage, dass dein Vater Blau mag.

Sage, dass du zwei Brüder hast.

Sage, dass dein Bruder Ben Rot nicht mag.

Sage, dass dein Bruder Steve Gelb mag.

My brother Steve likes yellow.

My father likes blue.

My brother Ben doesn't like red.

My mum is thirty-two years old.

I've got two brothers.

Time, numbers and colours

1 Read the words in the box and write the numbers.

2 Write the words in the puzzle.

forty-nine	thirty-two	eighteen	twenty-five
☐	☐	☐	☐

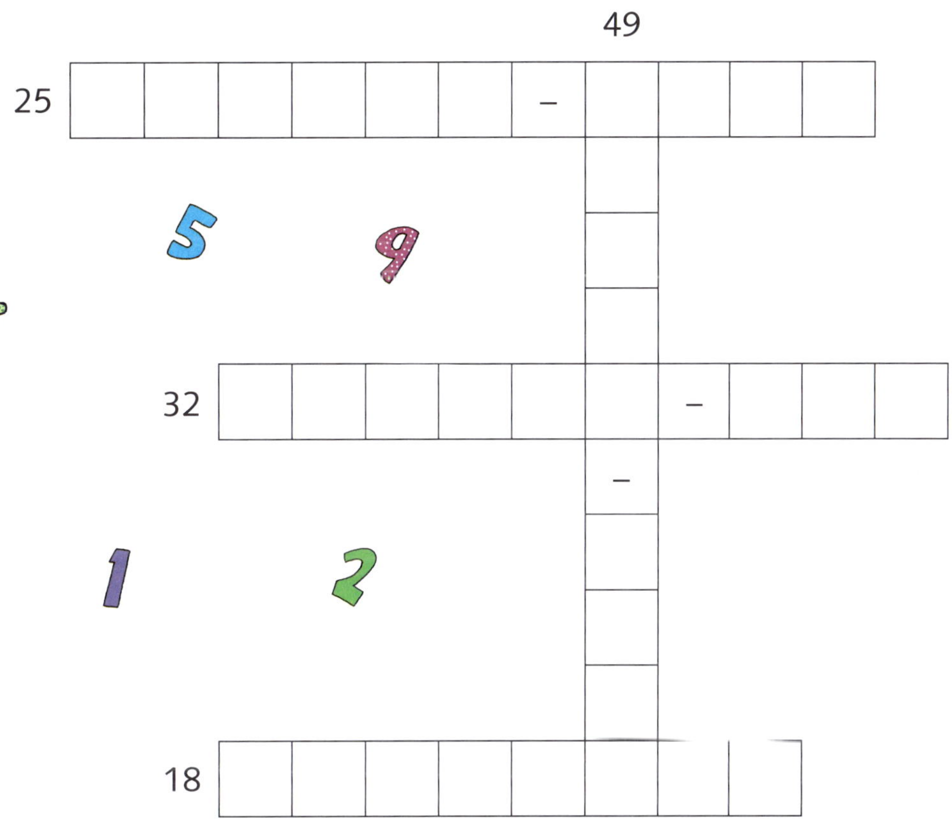

3 Match the words and the numbers. Draw lines.

sixty-four	17
twenty-eight	14
eleven	12
forty-one	11
seventeen	28
thirty-seven	64
fourteen	37
twelve	41

Time, numbers and colours

1 Count and colour.

2 Write the words in plural form.

~~red/hand~~ • blue/book • yellow/banana • brown/bag
grey/felt tip • black/shoe • green/apple

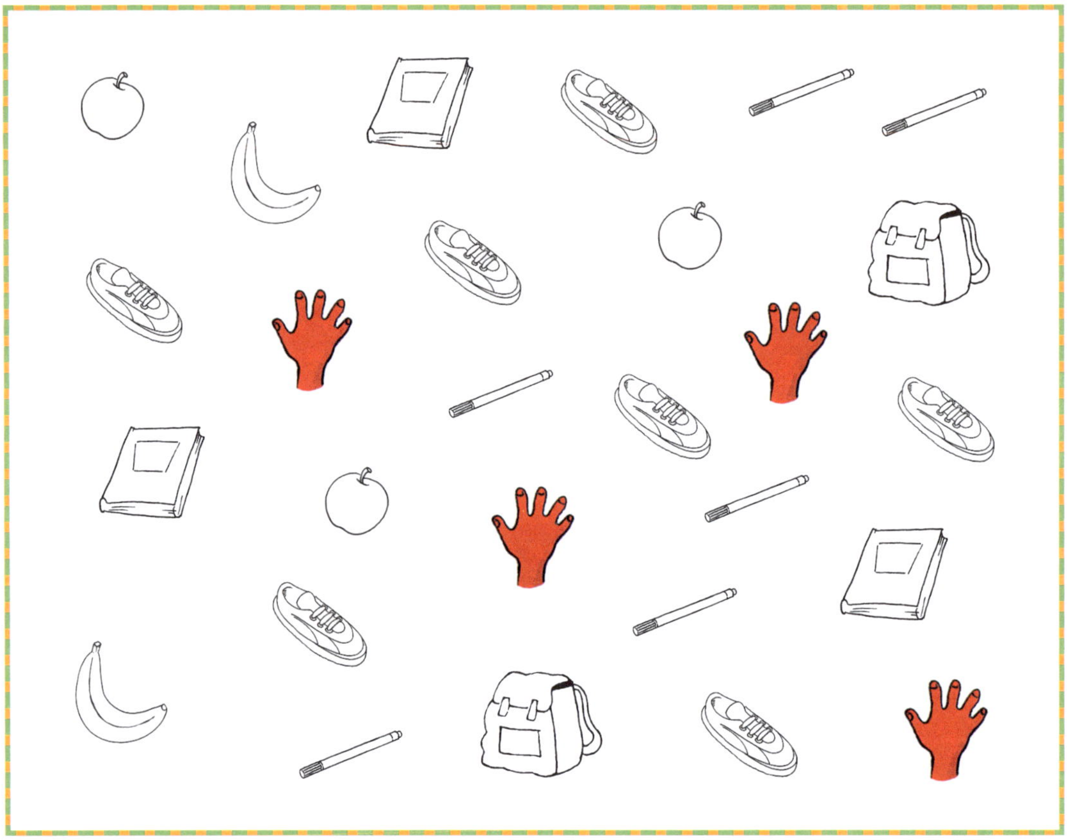

Four red hands

___________________ ___________________

___________________ ___________________

____

____

Note:
one shoe – two shoe**s**

Time, numbers and colours

1 How much is it? Write the sentences.

It's twenty-seven pounds.

It's ______________

____

____

2 What time is it? Write the sentences.

1 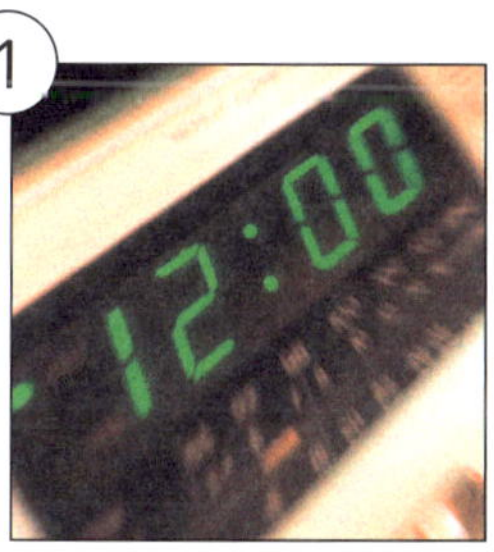

2 

3 

1 It's twelve o'clock.

2 It's ______________

3 ______________

Note: In England und in den USA ist die höchste Zahl für Uhrzeiten die 12.

4 

5 

6 

4 ______________

5 ______________

6 ______________

Time, numbers and colours

Note:
I have – he has
I play – he plays

1 What do the children do on Saturday?
Write the sentences.

I get up at eight o'clock.

get up 08:00

play a computer game 10:00

watch TV 07:00

go to bed 08:00

He gets up at nine o'clock.

get up 09:00

play with his dog 11:00

play football 05:00

have dinner 08:00

Time, numbers and colours

1 Which word doesn't fit? Find the odd one out.

museum • tower • motorbike • palace   motorbike

five • butterfly • eight • four

draw • write • find • kite

brother • twenty • thirty • forty

bus • museum • boat • taxi

fifty-one • fifty-two • seven • fifty-three

2 Match and number the speech bubbles.
Cross out the wrong ones.

1 Sage, dass Colin und Penny in London sind.

2 Sage, dass sie um neun Uhr mit dem Zug zum Museum fahren.

3 Sage, dass sie um vier Uhr mit dem Bus zum Zoo fahren.

4 Sage, dass sie am Big Ben zwölf Postkarten kaufen.

☐ At four o'clock they go to the zoo by bus.

☐ At four o'clock they go to Big Ben by boat.

1 Colin and Penny are in London.

☐ They buy twelve postcards at Big Ben.

☐ At twelve o'clock they go to the museum by bus.

☐ At nine o'clock they go to the museum by train.

Which two English sentences are wrong?

Seasons, months and days

1 Find 7 words and circle them. Look → and look ↓.

2 Write the words.

S	U	M	M	E	R	T	Z	U
G	N	K	L	B	Y	H	R	A
S	P	R	I	N	G	U	U	J
T	W	I	N	T	E	R	I	U
Z	E	W	R	C	A	S	E	L
F	E	D	M	O	N	D	A	Y
X	A	P	R	I	L	A	P	J
A	U	T	U	M	N	Y	R	P

seasons:
spring
____
____
____

months:
____
____

days:
____
____

Monday
summer
July
~~spring~~
autumn
Thursday
winter
April

3 Which months with J do you know?

J U N E, __________ ____________________

4 What season do they belong to?

_______ and ______ are in __________ January is in __________

5 Which month is it? Fill in the missing letters.

6 Write the solution word.

				T		M	B		
	A				S				
						C	H		
				M	A	Y			
	C		O						
					P			L	

Solution: | | | | | | |

Note: Wochentage und Monate werden auf Englisch groß geschrieben.

Seasons, months and days

1 Match the words. Draw lines.

1 reading — books

2 playing

3 watching

4 listening

5 meeting

badminton

friends

books

TV

to music

I like …

Note:
I like – she likes

2 What does Mia like? Write the word pairs and the sentences.

1 reading books — Mia likes reading books.

2 playing ______________ — Mia likes ______________

3 ______________ — ______________

4 ______________ — ______________

5 ______________ — ______________

3 What's Mia doing in her week?
Look at the numbers and write the sentences.

On Monday Mia is reading a book.

On Wednesday she's ______________

____

____

____

On Sunday I'm swimming in the sea.

What are you doing on Sunday?

____

Seasons, months and days

1 Complete the speech bubbles.

favourite colour • a dog
great • playing tennis

Frage deinen Freund, wo er am Mittwoch ist.

Where are you on Wednesday?

On Wednesday I'm meeting my father. We're going to the museum.

Sage, dass du das toll findest.

That's ___________

You're right. Museums are just great. What about you?

Sage, dass du am Mittwoch Tennis spielst:

On Wednesday I'm ________________

I don't like tennis. My favourite sport is judo.

Frage ihn nach seiner Lieblingsfarbe:

What's your ____________________

Well, I like blue and yellow. But my favourite colour is red. Have you got a pet?

Sage, dass du einen Hund hast:

I've got ________

On Saturday I jump off the ground.

A trip to London

1 Find 5 words and circle them. Look → and look ↓.

2 Write the words.

W	B	M	A	B	T	V	D	Z
M	O	T	O	R	B	I	K	E
B	A	B	C	S	S	O	H	O
I	T	P	A	U	B	U	S	Q
K	U	T	R	A	I	N	V	X
E	I	O	W	H	E	Z	T	N

boat

____

____

____

____

____

3 Look at today's weather. Help London tourists.
Write the sentences.
You can find more weather words on page 36.

today's weather						
	yes	no	no	no	yes	yes
	no	no	no	no	yes	yes
	no	no	no	no	yes	yes
	no	no	no	no	yes	no
	no	yes	yes	yes	no	no

It's rainy today. Go by bus, train or car.

It's _______________ Go by _______________

It's _______________ Go _______________

_______________ _______________

_______________ _______________

A trip to London

1 Do you know the London sights? Write sentences.

Note:
there's one boat –
there are two boats

a clock | Big Ben | There's | on

There's a clock on Big Ben.

the | penguins | There | London Zoo | are | in

____

flags | There | Tower Bridge | are | on

____

people | There | Buckingham Palace | are | at

____

boats | There | River Thames | are | on | the

____

A trip to London

1 Find 6 words and circle them.

Shirthalshoesgbcapanlusockswatrouserstoklskirt

2 What's in your suitcase? Draw lines and write the words.

A trip to London

1 Find 4 words. Circle and write them.

lionbtmonkeyswkelephantbesolparrots

2 It or they? Write the sentences.

Note:
one animal – it's
two animals – they're

Where is the elephant? It's in number one.

Where is ________ ? ______________________________

Where are ____________ ? They're ____________________

Where ____

3 True or false? Tick the right answers.

	Yes	No
Monkeys live in the jungle.	✓	
Elephants live in the bush.		
Parrots live in the sea.		
Lions live in trees.		

A trip to London

1 Complete the speech bubbles.

Hi, where were you on holiday?

Sage, dass du in London warst.

I was in London.

How did you like it?

Sage, dass es toll war.

It was ____________

What was the weather like?

Sage, dass es sonnig war.

____

What's your favourite place in London?

Sage, dass du den Zoo magst.

____

I like the guards at Buckingham Palace.

At school

1 Find 6 words and circle them. Look → and look ↓.

2 Write the words.

R	U	B	B	E	R	M	P
U	U	K	R	L	N	W	E
L	G	H	D	A	P	E	N
E	P	J	B	T	I	A	C
R	V	E	Q	D	E	N	I
E	A	S	I	E	M	T	L
S	C	I	S	S	O	R	S
T	B	O	O	K	J	U	R

 scissors

 ____________

 ____________

 ____________

 ____________

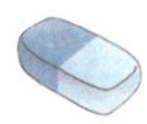 ____________

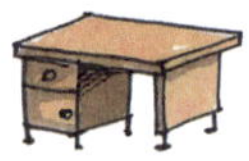 ____________

3 Match the word parts. Draw lines and write the words.

lunch	sharpener
felt	bag
pencil	stick
glue	case
school	tip
pencil	box

 lunch box

 ____________

 ____________

 ____________

 ____________

 ____________

4 Find the word pairs and write the words.

tirgh — Mia writes with her **left** hand. Max writes with his right hand.

kindr — In a supermarket you can buy **food** and ____________

eta — In a restaurant you can **drink** and ____________

lamsl — T-shirts can be **big** or ____________

I can be small, too.

At school

1 Count the school things and write the words.

two books

three ______________________

____

____

____

____

____

____

Note:
there is one pen –
there are many pens

2 What's in the pencil case? Count and write.

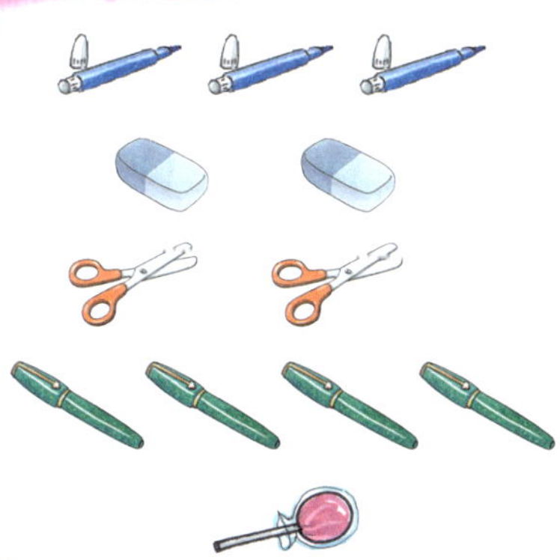

eftl stip	three felt tips
burbers	______________
sorsissc	______________
enps	______________
pollolip	______________

3 What's in your pencil case? Complete the sentence.

In my pencil case there is ______________________

and there are ______________________

____

____

At school

1 Complete the speech bubbles.

Do you like your school?

Sage, dass deine Schule ok ist.

My school is ok.

How many pupils are there in your class?

Sage, dass ihr 25 Schüler seid.

There are ______________ in our class.

How old is your teacher?

Sage, dass sie 35 ist.

____

Is she nice?

Sage, dass sie nett ist.

____

Have you got computers in your school?

Sage, dass in deinem Klassenzimmer drei Computer sind.

____
____
____

I've got a laptop at home.

Activities and body parts

1 Find 4 words and circle them. Look → and look ↓.

2 Write the words.

E	K	E	K	S	M	N	I
L	I	Q	T	W	G	L	N
E	N	G	L	I	S	H	T
P	E	T	K	M	Z	C	E
H	E	P	M	M	O	S	R
A	R	V	L	I	V	I	N
N	Q	C	P	N	T	S	E
T	W	X	M	G	S	I	T

 pet

 ______________

 ______________

 ______________

 ______________

3 Where should the children go?
Write the sentences.

computer room • ~~circus~~ • USA
swimming pool • pet shop

John and Mary like elephants. Go to the circus.

Max likes pets. Go to ______________

Lily and Dave like sports. Go to ______________

Ben likes the Internet. ______________

Maisie likes English. ______________

Note:
Internet wird auch auf Englisch groß geschrieben.

4 Draw a picture of your favourite activity.

Activities and body parts

1 What does your fantasy animal look like? Draw the body parts.

2 Write the words.

toe • ~~eye~~ • nose
arm • tooth • leg

My fantasy animal has got four eyes

____

____

____

____

Note:
one tooth –
two teeth

3 What does/doesn't your fantasy animal like?
Circle/cross out the words. Complete the sentences.

soup	parrots	playing tennis
spaghetti	monkeys	swimming
pizza	tigers	doing judo
ice cream	crocodiles	playing football

My fantasy animal likes ______________________________

It doesn't like ______________________________

____

4 What about you?
Write three or more things you like and don't like.

I like ______________________________

I don't like ______________________________

Activities and body parts

1 What's wrong with the children? Match and write.

I've got an earache. ______________

I've got a cough. ______________

I've got a headache. ______________

I've got a cold. ______________

I've got a tummy ache. ______________

I've got a sore throat. ______________

Note:
a tummy ache
an earache

2 What do they need? Write the sentences.

	I've got a cold.		Take six grey pills.
	I've got ______________		Take ______________
	I've got ______________		Take ______________
	I've ______________		______________
	______________	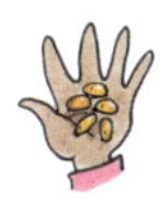	______________
	______________	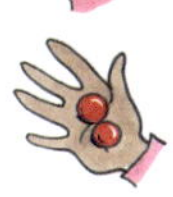	______________

Activities and body parts

1 Read Sophie's email.

Note:
Deutsch: E-Mail
Englisch: email

To:
Subject: E-pals

Hi,
How are you? I'm Sophie from New York. Let's be e-pals. I'm 10 years old. I live in Brooklyn, New York. We live in a small house. My father is a taxi driver. He has got a taxi. Taxis in New York are yellow. We call them cabs. My mother is a teacher. Her school is on Union Street, in the city center. I've got one brother and one sister. My brother is 18 and a student. My sister is only eight. My hobby is writing emails to children from all over the world. What about you?

Yours,
Sophie

2 Write an answer to Sophie's email.

- Begrüße deine E-Mail-Freundin.
- Frage sie, wie es ihr geht.
- Bedanke dich für ihre E-Mail.
- Du findest New York toll.
- Du würdest gerne das Empire State Building sehen.
- Schreibe, dass deine Mutter Polizistin ist.
- Schreibe, dass du zwei Brüder hast.
- Verabschiede dich.

To:
Subject: E-pals

_____ How __________ Thank you ____________________

______________________ I would like to ______________

______________________________ My mum ____________

____________________ I've got ______________________

____

Food and shopping

1 Find 7 words and circle them. Look → and look ↓.

2 Write the words.

S	A	N	D	W	I	C	H	D
O	H	L	C	K	J	I	A	H
U	T	L	U	W	J	T	M	U
P	I	Z	Z	A	U	B	B	J
L	A	G	D	T	O	G	U	U
M	I	Z	T	E	A	W	R	I
L	B	C	J	R	E	G	G	C
C	O	L	A	S	O	F	E	E
H	O	M	L	U	P	L	R	W

Food

sandwich

____

____

____

Drink

____

____

____

____

Note:
I'd like = I would like

3 What would you like? Order your lunch.
Write the sentences.

I'd like spaghetti and a cola, please.

I'd like ____________________ and ________________________, please.

I'd like ______________________
____

____
____

Food and shopping

1 What has Ben got for lunch? What has Jane got? Tick/cross out. Write the sentences.

Note:
he's got = he has got
she hasn't got = she has not got

He's got a hamburger.

He hasn't got a ______

He's got ______

He ______

She's got spaghetti.

She hasn't got ______

She's got ______

She ______

Note:
I can't = I can not

2 What can they do with 5 pounds? Complete the sentences.

He ______ drink apple juice. He ______ eat pizza.

He ______ buy the pocket knife. ______

______

She ______ buy the book. ______

______

Food and shopping

1 What would they like? Read the sentences.

2 Complete the speech bubbles.

Hi. Have you got a green rubber, please? • That's 80 pence, please.
I'd like a red T-shirt, please. • Have you got cherry ice cream?
Anything else? • Sorry, we haven't got cherry ice cream.

Food and shopping

1 Write the words into the right boxes.

2 Cross out the wrong words.

rat • ~~sight~~ • tennis • rabbit • pupil •dog • grandma
knee • banana • nose • sandwich • hand • toe • pizza • apple
soup • football • volleyball • guinea pig • book
hamster • basketball • partner •judo • birthday • teacher
swimming • mother • cat • morning

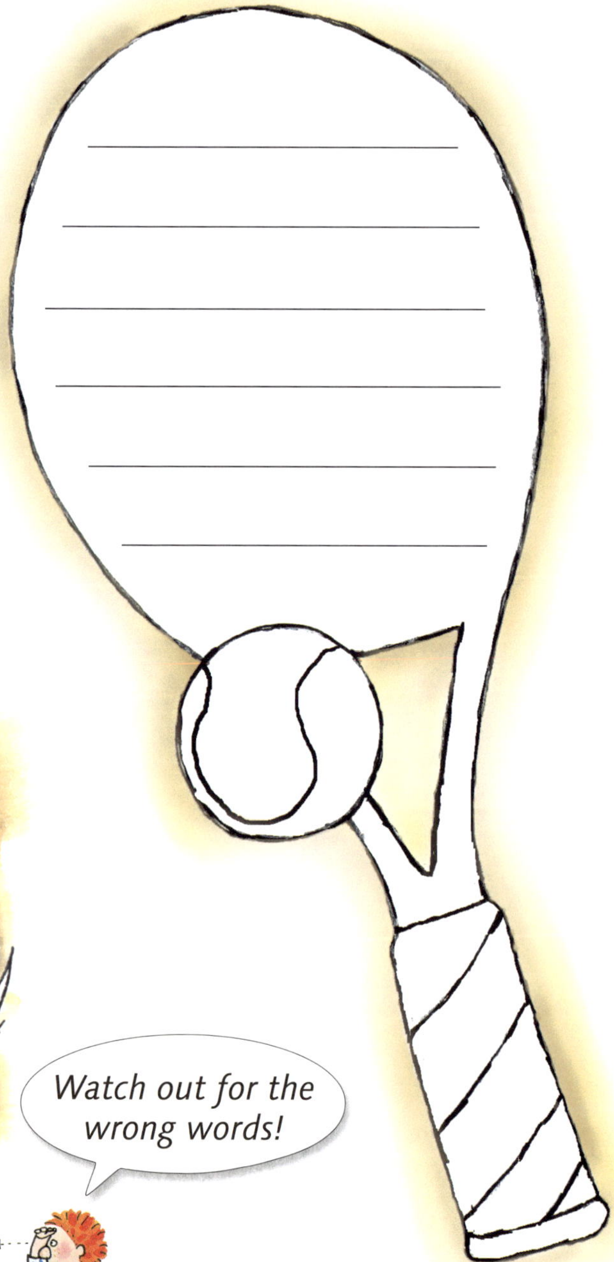

Word fields

Family

brother Bruder
brothers and sisters Geschwister
father/dad Vater/Papa
grandfather/grandpa Großvater/Opa
grandmother/grandma Großmutter/Oma
mother/mum Mutter/Mama
sister Schwester

More words:

Have you got brothers or sisters? I've got two brothers.

Colours

black schwarz
blue blau
brown braun
green grün
grey grau
pink rosa
red rot
white weiß
yellow gelb

More words:

What colour is your T-shirt? It's green.

Months and days

January Januar
February Februar
March März
April April
May Mai
June Juni
July Juli
August August
September September
October Oktober
November November
December Dezember

Monday Montag
Tuesday Dienstag
Wednesday Mittwoch
Thursday Donnerstag
Friday Freitag
Saturday Samstag
Sunday Sonntag

When's your birthday? It's in January.

Word fields

Seasons and the weather

cloudy bewölkt
foggy nebelig
rainy regnerisch 
snowy verschneit
sunny sonnig 
windy windig

spring Frühling 
summer Sommer
autumn Herbst
winter Winter 

More words:

____

____

January is in winter.
What's the weather like in summer? It's often sunny in summer.

Time and numbers

1 one
2 two
3 three
4 four
5 five
6 six
7 seven
8 eight
9 nine
10 ten

11 eleven
12 twelve
13 thirteen
14 fourteen
15 fifteen
16 sixteen
17 seventeen
18 eighteen
19 nineteen

20 twenty, **21** twenty-one, … **29** twenty-nine
30 thirty, **31** thirty-one, … **39** thirty-nine
40 forty, **41** forty-one, … **49** forty-nine
50 fifty, **51** fifty-one, … **59** fifty-nine 59
60 sixty, **61** sixty-one, … **69** sixty-nine
70 seventy, **71** seventy-one, … **79** seventy-nine
80 eighty, **81** eighty-one, … **89** eighty-nine
90 ninety, **91** ninety-one, … **99** ninety-nine
100 a/one hundred 100

What time is it?
It's seven o'clock.

More words:

____

____

Word fields

London transport

bike Fahrrad
boat Boot
bus Bus

car Auto
motorbike Motorrad

train Zug

More words:

____

____

Where were you on holiday? I was in London.

Clothes

cap Mütze
shirt Hemd
shoes Schuhe
skirt Rock
socks Socken

trousers Hose

More words:

____

____

What's in your suitcase? In my suitcase, there are trousers and my favourite shirt.

Pets and wild animals

cat Katze
crocodile Krokodil
dog Hund
elephant Elefant
guinea pig Meerschweinchen
hamster Hamster
lion Löwe
monkey Affe
parrot Papagei

penguin Pinguin
pet Haustier

More words:

____

____

Have you got a pet? Yes, I've got a dog./No, I haven't.

Word fields

School

book Buch 
desk Schreibtisch
felt tip Filzstift 
glue stick Klebstift
lunch box Brotdose
pen Füller 
pencil Bleistift 
pencil case Federtasche
pencil sharpener Bleistiftspitzer
rubber Radiergummi 
ruler Lineal
school bag Schultasche 
scissors Schere

More words:

____

____

What's in your pencil case? There's a ruler and a rubber.

Activities

badminton Badminton 
basketball Basketball
judo, doing judo Judo, Judo betreiben
listening to music Musik hören 
play spielen
playing computer games Computerspiele spielen 
playing football Fußball spielen
reading lesen 
swimming schwimmen
Let's go swimming.
tennis Tennis 
watching TV fernsehen
yoga, doing yoga Yoga, Yoga machen

More words:

____

____

What's your favourite free-time activity?
My favourite free-time activity is playing football.

Word fields

Body

arm Arm
cold Erkältung
cough Husten
earache Ohrenschmerzen
eye Auge

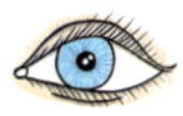

headache Kopfschmerzen
leg Bein
nose Nase

sore throat Halsschmerzen
tooth, teeth Zahn, Zähne

toe Zeh
tummy ache Bauchschmerzen

More words:

____

____

What's wrong with you? I've got a headache.

Food and drink

apple Apfel

banana Banane
cola Cola
cup, a cup of tea Tasse, eine Tasse Tee
glass, a glass of cola Glas, ein Glas Cola
hamburger Hamburger
ice cream Eiscreme

juice Saft
lollipop Lutscher

pizza Pizza
sandwich Sandwich
soup Suppe
spaghetti Spaghetti
tea Tee
water Wasser

More words:

____

____

What would you like to drink? I'd like some water, please.

Let's talk

Du möchtest jemanden besser kennenlernen:

Where are you from?
How old are you?
What's your favourite colour/sport/…?
What are your favourite pets/…?

What's your favourite food?

Du möchtest dich vorstellen:

That's me/my family.
I've got two brothers/one sister/…
I haven't got any brothers and sisters.
My mom/grandpa/dad is … years old.
This is …
I'm from …
I'm … years old.
My favourite … are/is …
I like …

I'm from Berlin.

Du möchtest nach der Uhrzeit fragen und über deinen Tag sprechen:

What time is it? It's …
I get up at … o'clock./I go to bed at … o'clock.

Du möchtest über das Wetter sprechen:

What's the weather like today/in London?
Today it's rainy/sunny/cloudy/…

Du möchtest im Restaurant etwas bestellen/etwas einkaufen:

What would you like?
I'd like a …
Do you have …?
I can/can't buy/eat/go to …
How much is it? It's … pounds/euro.

I'd like a cola.

Du möchtest über die Ferien sprechen:

Where were you on holiday?
I was in …
What did you like best?
What's your favourite …?

What's your favourite sight in London?

Fragewörter

How? Wie? **When?** Wann?
What? Was ? **Where?** Wo?

Solutions

Me and my friends

1 Find 5 words and circle them. Look → and look ↓.

2 Write the words.

T	P	G	R	E	E	N	L
E	F	R	U	L	K	I	T
N	O	M	L	I	L	Y	K
N	N	K	O	N	R	I	S
I	T	K	L	D	O	G	K
S	E	N	P	L	I	N	R
E	N	G	L	A	N	D	T

Lily

England

green

tennis

10 ten

dog

3 Look at the crossword and complete the sentences.

4 Draw your friend.

Note: she's = she is

Her name is Lily.

She's from England.

She's ten years old.

Her favourite sport is tennis.

Her favourite colour is green.

Her favourite pet is the dog.

She's my friend.

three 3

Me and my friends

1 Complete the speech bubbles.

2 Glue on or draw the pictures.

3 Write the names.

Note: I'm = I am

That's me.

My favourite colour is ______

I'm ____ years old.

I'm from ______

My favourite sport is ______

name: ______

That's my friend.

Her favourite colour is ______

She's ____ years old.

She's from ______

Her favourite sport is ______

name: ______

Hi, I'm Ginger.

4 four

Me and my friends

1 Write the sentences.

2 Complete the speech bubbles. Look on page 3.

Note: what's = what is

your/What's/name?

What's your name?

My name is Lily.

from/are/Where/you?

Where are you from?

I'm from England.

old/How/you/are?

How old are you?

I'm ten years old.

your/favourite/What's/sport?

What's your favourite sport?

My favourite sport is tennis.

favourite/What's/pet/your?

What's your favourite pet?

My favourite pet is the dog.

colour/What's /favourite/your?

What's your favourite colour?

My favourite colour is green.

3 Write one sentence about yourself.

I'm from England. What about you?

five 5

My family

1 Find 5 words and circle them. Look → and look ↓.

2 Write the words.

U	I	D	O	P	G	X	H	I	M	P
S	W	J	S	B	R	O	T	H	E	R
I	P	A	X	F	A	T	H	E	R	H
S	B	T	N	M	N	E	R	Z	L	Z
T	G	R	A	N	D	P	A	H	P	B
E	U	A	K	O	M	O	T	H	E	R
R	U	M	A	K	A	J	O	D	E	X

father • mother • ~~grandpa~~ grandma • brother • sister

grandpa

father

grandma

mother

brother

sister

Note: grandpa = grandfather, grandma = grandmother

3 Look at Karen's family. Complete the sentences.

This is John, my grandpa.

This is Linda, my grandma.

This is Lucy, my grandma.

This is Bill, my grandpa.

This is Jenny, my mother.

This is Tom, my father.

This is Emma, my sister.

Hi, I'm Karen. This is my family.

This is Ben, my brother.

6 six

Solutions

My family

1 Tick the right answers.

	Yes	No
Bill is Karen's grandpa.	✓	
John is Karen's father.		✓
Emma is Karen's sister.	✓	
Jenny is Karen's mother.	✓	
Lucy is Karen's sister.		✓
Ben is Karen's brother.	✓	

2 Make sentences about Karen's family. Draw lines.

Jenny, Bill, Lucy, Emma, Ben, Tom, Linda, John, Charlie — is Karen's — father, mother, sister, brother, grandpa, grandma, dog

3 He or she? Write the family words.

Note: my dog Charlie = he, a dog = it

grandpa	
father	grandma
brother	mother
Charlie, the dog	sister

My family

1 Who is who in Karen's family? Look on page 6. Number the pictures.

2 Write the sentences.

1 This is my grandpa Bill. He's 65.

2 This is my sister Emma. She's 8.

3 This is my father Tom. He's 33.

4 This is my grandma Lucy. She's 63.

5 This is my mother Jenny. She's 32.

6 This is my brother Ben. He's 14.

7 This is my grandma Linda. She's 68.

8 This is my grandpa John. He's 67.

3 Who is missing? Write the sentence and number the picture.

9 This is my dog Charlie. He's 2.

4 Complete the drawing.

My family

1 Find 5 words and colour them.

Bluelaredilgreenbnblackipyellowrn

2 Write the words.

3 Do you know one more? Colour and write.

green, yellow, blue, red, black, ______

4 Tick the right answers.

	bananas are yellow	shamrocks are green	cola is brown	the sun is blue	crocodiles are red
Yes	✓	✓	✓		
No				✓	✓

5 Colour the pictures.

6 Write the sentences.

Note: they are – they aren't, it is – it isn't

Yes, bananas are yellow.

No, the sun isn't blue. It is yellow.

No, crocodiles aren't red. They are green.

Yes, shamrocks are green.

Yes, cola is brown.

My family

1 Complete the sentences.

2 Write the numbers in the boxes.

under • on • behind • in
yellow • brown • pink • ~~black~~

1 The black cat is behind the chair.

2 The yellow cheese is on the sandwich.

3 The brown dog is under the table.

4 The pink flower is in the glass.

3 Match the sentences. Draw lines.

- Sage, dass deine Mutter 32 Jahre alt ist. — My mum is thirty-two years old.
- Sage, dass dein Vater Blau mag. — My father likes blue.
- Sage, dass du zwei Brüder hast. — I've got two brothers.
- Sage, dass dein Bruder Ben Rot nicht mag. — My brother Ben doesn't like red.
- Sage, dass dein Bruder Steve Gelb mag. — My brother Steve likes yellow.

Solutions

Time, numbers and colours

1 Read the words in the box and write the numbers.

2 Write the words in the puzzle.

forty-nine	thirty-two	eighteen	twenty-five
49	32	18	25

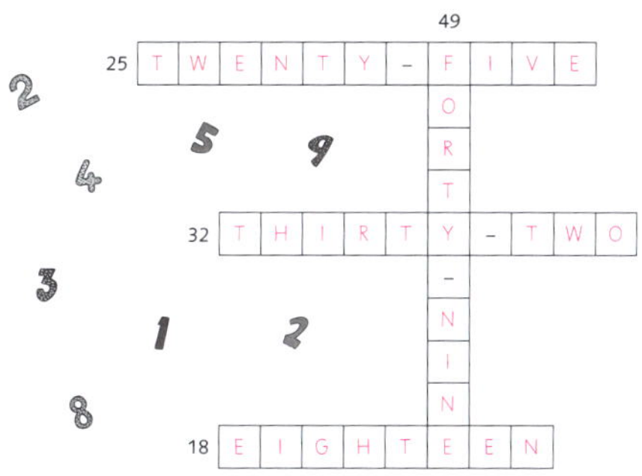

3 Match the words and the numbers. Draw lines.

sixty-four	17
twenty-eight	14
eleven	12
forty-one	11
seventeen	28
thirty-seven	64
fourteen	37
twelve	41

Time, numbers and colours

1 Count and colour.

2 Write the words in the plural form.

~~red/hand~~ • blue/book • yellow/banana • brown/bag
grey/felt tip • black/shoe • green/apple

Four red hands

three blue books — seven black shoes

two yellow bananas — three green apples

two brown bags

six grey felt tips

Note: one shoe – two shoes

Time, numbers and colours

1 How much is it? Write the sentences.

It's twenty-seven pounds. — It's five pounds. — It's thirty-three pounds. — It's eighty-five pounds.

2 What time is it? Write the sentences.

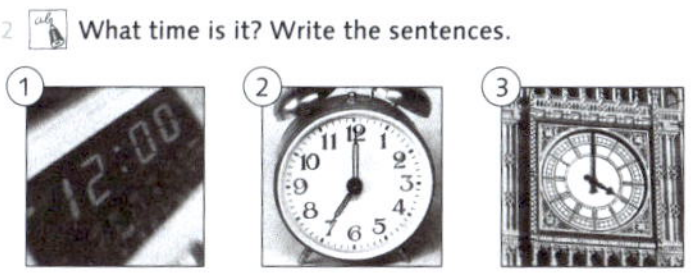

1 It's twelve o'clock.

2 It's seven o'clock.

3 It's four o'clock.

Note: In England und in den USA ist die höchste Zahl für Uhrzeiten die 12.

4 It's eight o'clock.

5 It's three o'clock.

6 It's one o'clock.

Time, numbers and colours

1 What do the children do on Saturday? Write the sentences.

Note: I have – he has; I play – he plays

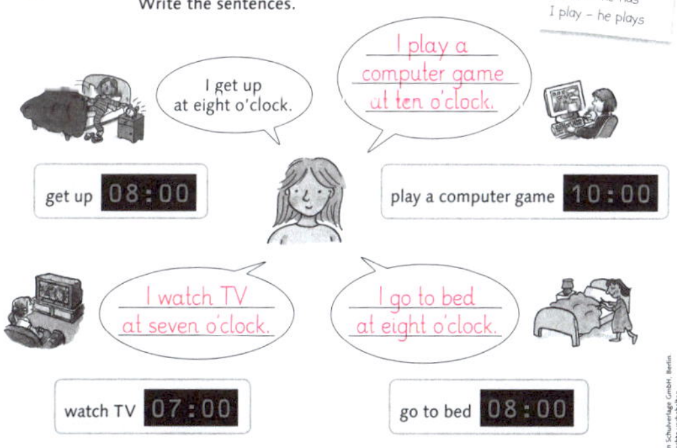

Solutions

Time, numbers and colours

1 Which word doesn't fit? Find the odd one out.

museum • tower • (motorbike) • palace	motorbike
five • (butterfly) • eight • four	butterfly
draw • write • find • (kite)	kite
(brother) • twenty • thirty • forty	brother
bus • (museum) • boat • taxi	museum
fifty-one • fifty-two • (seven) • fifty-three	seven

2 Match and number the speech bubbles. Cross out the wrong ones.

① Sage, dass Colin und Penny in London sind.

② Sage, dass sie um neun Uhr mit dem Zug zum Museum fahren.

③ Sage, dass sie um vier Uhr mit dem Bus zum Zoo fahren.

④ Sage, dass sie am Big Ben zwölf Postkarten kaufen.

- [3] At four o'clock they go to the zoo by bus.
- [ ] ~~At four o'clock they go to Big Ben by boat.~~
- [1] Colin and Penny are in London.
- [4] They buy twelve postcards at Big Ben.
- [ ] ~~At twelve o'clock they go to the museum by bus.~~
- [2] At nine o'clock they go to the museum by train.

Which two English sentences are wrong?

Seasons, months and days

1 Find 7 words and circle them. Look → and look ↓.

2 Write the words.

S	U	M	M	E	R	T	Z	U
G	N	K	L	B	Y	H	R	A
S	P	R	I	N	G	U	U	J
T	W	I	N	T	E	R	I	U
Z	E	W	R	C	A	S	E	L
F	E	D	M	O	N	D	A	Y
X	A	P	R	I	L	A	P	J
A	U	T	U	M	N	Y	R	P

seasons: spring, summer, autumn, winter

months: April, July

days: Monday, Thursday

Monday
summer
July
~~spring~~
autumn
Thursday
winter
April

3 Which months with J do you know?

JUNE, JULY, JANUARY

4 What season do they belong to?

June and July are in summer. January is in winter.

5 Which month is it? Fill in the missing letters.

6 Write the solution word.

	S	E	P	T	E	M	B	E	R
	A	U	G	U	S	T			
			M	A	R	C	H		
				M	A	Y			
O	C	T	O	B	E	R			
				A	P	R	I	L	

Solution: S U M M E R

Note: Wochentage und Monate werden auf Englisch groß geschrieben.

In which season is Easter?

Seasons, months and days

1 Match the words. Draw lines.

[1] reading — books
[2] playing — badminton
[3] watching — TV
[4] listening — to music
[5] meeting — friends

I like …

Note: I like – she likes

2 What does Mia like? Write the word pairs and the sentences.

1	reading books	Mia likes reading books.
2	playing badminton	Mia likes playing badminton.
3	watching TV	Mia likes watching TV.
4	listening to music	Mia likes listening to music.
5	meeting friends	Mia likes meeting friends.

3 What's Mia doing in her week? Look at the numbers and write the sentences.

Mon 1 — On Monday Mia is reading a book.

Wed 3 — On Wednesday she's watching TV.

Fri 5 — On Friday she's meeting friends.

Thur 4 — On Thursday she's listening to music.

Tues 2 — On Tuesday she's playing badminton.

On Sunday I'm swimming in the sea.

What are you doing on Sunday?

____

Seasons, months and days

1 Complete the speech bubbles.

favourite colour • a dog
great • playing tennis

Frage deinen Freund, wo er am Mittwoch ist.

Where are you on Wednesday?

On Wednesday I'm meeting my father. We're going to the museum.

Sage, dass du das toll findest.

That's great.

You're right. Museums are just great. What about you?

Sage, dass du am Mittwoch Tennis spielst:

On Wednesday I'm playing tennis.

I don't like tennis. My favourite sport is judo.

Frage ihn nach seiner Lieblingsfarbe:

What's your favourite colour?

Well, I like blue and yellow. But my favourite colour is red. Have you got a pet?

Sage, dass du einen Hund hast:

I've got a dog.

On Saturday I jump off the ground.

Solutions

A trip to London

1 Find 5 words and circle them. Look → and look ↓.

2 Write the words.

W	B	M	A	B	T	V	D	Z
M	O	T	O	R	B	I	K	E
B	A	B	C	S	S	O	H	O
I	T	P	A	U	B	U	S	Q
K	U	T	R	A	I	N	V	X
E	I	O	W	H	E	Z	T	N

boat
car
bike
bus
motorbike
train

3 Look at today's weather. Help London tourists. Write the sentences. You can find more weather words on page 36.

today's weather						
	yes	no	no	no	yes	yes
	no	no	no	no	yes	yes
	no	no	no	no	yes	yes
	no	no	no	no	yes	no
	no	yes	yes	yes	no	no

It's rainy today. Go by bus, train or car.

It's windy today. Go by train or car.

It's cloudy today. Go by train or car.

It's snowy today. Go by train.

It's sunny today. Go by boat, motorbike or bike.

A trip to London

1 Do you know the London sights? Write sentences.

Note: there's one boat – there are two boats

a clock | Big Ben | There's | on

There's a clock on Big Ben.

the penguins | There | London Zoo | are | in

There are penguins in the London Zoo.

flags | There | Tower Bridge | are | on

There are flags on Tower Bridge.

people | There | Buckingham Palace | are | at

There are people at Buckingham Palace.

boats | There | River Thames | are | on | the

There are boats on the River Thames.

A trip to London

1 Find 6 words and circle them.

Shirthalshoesgbcapunlusockswatrouseratuklskirt

2 What's in your suitcase? Draw lines and write the words.

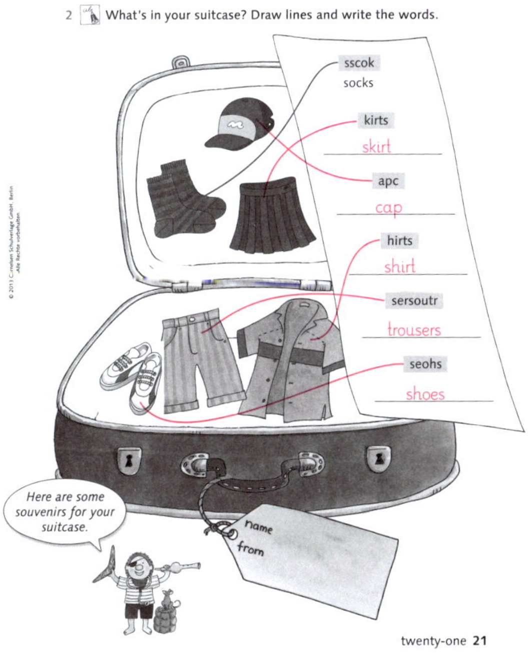

sscok – socks
kirts – skirt
apc – cap
hirts – shirt
sersoutr – trousers
seohs – shoes

A trip to London

1 Find 4 words. Circle and write them.

lionbtmonkeyswkelephantbesolparrots

2 It or they? Write the sentences.

Note: one animal – it's; two animals – they're

Where is the elephant? It's in number one.

Where is the lion ? It's in number four.

Where are the monkeys ? They're in number two.

Where are the parrots? They're in number three.

3 True or false? Tick the right answers.

	Yes	No
Monkeys live in the jungle.	✓	
Elephants live in the bush.	✓	
Parrots live in the sea.		✓
Lions live in trees.		✓

Solutions

A trip to London

1 Complete the speech bubbles.

Hi, where were you on holiday?

Sage, dass du in London warst.

I was in London.

How did you like it?

Sage, dass es toll war.

It was great.

What was the weather like?

Sage, dass es sonnig war.

It was sunny.

What's your favourite place in London?

Sage, dass du den Zoo magst.

I like the zoo.

I like the guards at Buckingham Palace.

At school

1 Find 6 words and circle them. Look → and look ↓.

2 Write the words.

R	U	B	B	E	R	M	P
U	U	K	R	L	N	W	E
L	G	H	D	A	P	E	N
E	P	J	B	T	I	A	C
R	V	E	Q	D	E	N	I
E	A	S	I	E	M	T	L
S	C	I	S	S	O	R	S
T	B	O	O	K	J	U	R

scissors
ruler
book
pen
pencil
rubber
desk

3 Match the word parts. Draw lines and write the words.

lunch	sharpener
felt	bag
pencil	stick
glue	case
school	tip
pencil	box

lunch box
felt tip
pencil case
glue stick
school bag
pencil sharpener

4 Find the word pairs and write the words.

tirgh — Mia writes with her **left** hand. Max writes with his right hand.

kindr — In a supermarket you can buy **food** and drink.

eta — In a restaurant you can **drink** and eat.

lamsl — T-shirts can be **big** or small.

I can be small, too.

At school

1 Count the school things and write the words.

two books
three pencil cases
six felt tips
four rulers
five pencils
two lunch boxes
two school bags
three rubbers

Note: there is one pen – there are many pens

2 What's in the pencil case? Count and write.

eftl stip	three felt tips
burbers	two rubbers
sorsissc	two scissors
enps	four pens
pollolip	one lollipop

3 What's in your pencil case? Complete the sentence.

In my pencil case there is ______

and there are ______

Where's my pencil case?

At school

1 Complete the speech bubbles.

Do you like your school?

Sage, dass deine Schule ok ist.

My school is ok.

How many pupils are there in your class?

Sage, dass ihr 25 Schüler seid.

There are 25 pupils in our class.

How old is your teacher?

Sage, dass sie 35 ist.

She's 35.

Is she nice?

Sage, dass sie nett ist.

Yes, she's nice.

Have you got computers in your school?

Sage, dass in deinem Klassenzimmer drei Computer sind.

There are three computers in my classroom.

I've got a laptop at home.

Solutions

Activities and body parts

1 Find 4 words and circle them. Look → and look ↓.

2 Write the words.

E	K	E	K	S	M	N	I
L	I	Q	T	W	G	L	N
E	N	G	L	I	S	H	T
P	E	T	K	M	Z	C	E
H	E	P	M	M	O	S	R
A	R	V	L	I	V	I	N
N	Q	C	P	N	T	S	E
T	W	X	M	G	S	I	T

pet
English
elephant
swimming
Internet

3 Where should the children go? Write the sentences.

computer room • ~~circus~~ • USA
swimming pool • pet shop

John and Mary like elephants. Go to the circus.
Max likes pets. Go to the pet shop.
Lily and Dave like sports. Go to the swimming pool.
Ben likes the Internet. Go to the computer room.
Maisie likes English. Go to the USA.

Note: Internet wird auch auf Englisch groß geschrieben.

4 Draw a picture of your favourite activity.

My favourite activity is eating ice cream.

twenty-seven 27

Activities and body parts

1 What does your fantasy animal look like? Draw the body parts.

2 Write the words.

toe • ~~eye~~ • nose
arm • tooth • leg

My fantasy animal has got four eyes

Note: one tooth – two teeth

3 What does/doesn't your fantasy animal like? Circle/cross out the words. Complete the sentences.

soup	parrots	playing tennis
spaghetti	monkeys	swimming
pizza	tigers	doing judo
ice cream	crocodiles	playing football

My fantasy animal likes ______
It doesn't like ______

4 What about you? Write three or more things you like and don't like.

I like singing.

I like ______
I don't like ______

28 twenty-eight

Activities and body parts

1 What's wrong with the children? Match and write.

I've got an earache. – David
I've got a cough. – Clara
I've got a headache. – Peter
I've got a cold. – Elsa
I've got a tummy ache. – Nelson
I've got a sore throat. – Marvin

Note: a tummy ache, an earache

2 What do they need? Write the sentences.

I've got a cold.	Take six grey pills.
I've got an earache.	Take one blue pill.
I've got a tummy ache.	Take four orange pills.
I've got a cough.	Take three green pills.
I've got a sore throat.	Take five yellow pills.
I've got a headache	Take two red pills.

twenty-nine 29

Activities and body parts

1 Read Sophie's email.

To:
Subject: E-pals

Hi,
How are you? I'm Sophie from New York. Let's be e-pals. I'm 10 years old. I live in Brooklyn, New York. We live in a small house. My father is a taxi driver. He has got a taxi. Taxis in New York are yellow. We call them cabs. My mother is a teacher. Her school is on Union Street, in the city center. I've got one brother and one sister. My brother is 18 and a student. My sister is only eight. My hobby is writing emails to children from all over the world. What about you?

Yours,
Sophie

Note: Deutsch: E-Mail, Englisch: email

Hi, let's be e-pals.

2 Write an answer to Sophie's email.

- Begrüße deine E-Mail-Freundin.
- Frage sie, wie es ihr geht.
- Bedanke dich für ihre E-Mail.
- Du findest New York toll.
- Du würdest gerne das Empire State Building sehen.
- Schreibe, dass deine Mutter Polizistin ist.
- Schreibe, dass du zwei Brüder hast.
- Verabschiede dich.

To:
Subject: E-pals

Hi! How are you? Thank you for your email. New York is great. I would like to see the Empire State Building. My mum is a police officer. I've got two brothers. Bye.

30 thirty

Solutions

Food and shopping

1 Find 7 words and circle them. Look → and look ↓.

2 Write the words.

S	A	N	D	W	I	C	H	D
O	H	L	C	K	J	I	A	H
U	T	L	U	W	J	T	M	U
P	I	Z	Z	A	U	B	B	J
L	A	G	D	T	O	G	U	U
M	I	Z	T	E	A	W	R	I
L	B	C	J	R	E	G	G	C
C	O	L	A	S	O	F	E	E
H	O	M	L	U	P	L	R	W

Note: I'd like = I would like

Food
sandwich
hamburger
soup
pizza

Drink
water
cola
juice
tea

3 What would you like? Order your lunch. Write the sentences.

Spaghetti, a cola — I'd like spaghetti and a cola, please.

two hamburgers, some water — I'd like two hamburgers and some water, please.

a sandwich, a cup of tea — I'd like a sandwich and a cup of tea, please.

pizza, a glass of juice — I'd like pizza and a glass of juice, please.

I'd like some tea, please!

thirty-one 31

Food and shopping

1 What has Ben got for lunch? What has Jane got? Tick/cross out. Write the sentences.

Note: he's got = he has got; she hasn't got = she has not got

Menu: hamburger, ~~sandwich~~, water, cola

He's got a hamburger.
He hasn't got a sandwich.
He's got water.
He hasn't got cola.

I've got a big tummy.

Menu: spaghetti, pizza, tea, cola

She's got spaghetti.
She hasn't got pizza.
She's got cola.
She hasn't got tea.

Note: I can't = I can not

2 What can they do with 5 pounds? Complete the sentences.

He can drink apple juice. He can't eat pizza.

He can't buy the pocket knife. He can buy the water bottle.

She can buy the book. She can buy the ruler.

32 thirty-two

Food and shopping

1 What would they like? Read the sentences.

2 Complete the speech bubbles.

Hi. Have you got a green rubber, please? • That's 80 pence, please. I'd like a red T-shirt, please. • Have you got cherry ice cream? Anything else? • Sorry, we haven't got cherry ice cream.

I'd like a red T-shirt, please.

A red T-shirt? Here you are. Anything else?

No, thank you.

Hi. Have you got a green rubber, please?

A green rubber? Yes, here you are. That's 80 pence, please.

Have you got cherry ice cream?

Sorry, we haven't got cherry ice cream.

What about orange ice cream?

thirty-three 33

Food and shopping

1 Write the words into the right boxes.

2 Cross out the wrong words.

rat • ~~sight~~ • tennis • rabbit • ~~pupil~~ • dog • ~~grandma~~ • ~~knee~~ • banana • ~~nose~~ • sandwich • ~~hand~~ • ~~toe~~ • pizza • apple • soup • football • volleyball • guinea pig • ~~book~~ • hamster • basketball • ~~partner~~ • judo • ~~birthday~~ • ~~teacher~~ • swimming • ~~mother~~ • cat • ~~morning~~

apple, banana, sandwich, pizza, soup

judo, tennis, basketball, swimming, volleyball, football

rat, cat, hamster, guinea pig, rabbit, dog

Watch out for the wrong words!

34 thirty-four